Advance praise for Children Shouldn't Use Knives and Other Tales

"*Children Shouldn't Use Knives and Other Tales* is like bittersweet chocolate, darkly evocative and tender-tough in its imaginings. Shirley Camia's scant, spare words, interpretatively arrayed with Cindy Mochizuki's visual musings and prefaced with excerpts from well-known children's writers, provide the reader with a truly rich reading experience."

— Sally Ito, author of *Alert to Glory*

"If childhood were a room, Shirley Camia's *Children Shouldn't Use Knives and Other Tales* paces off the corners, fiddles with the light switch and breaks the blinds. Camia writes 'the dawn has a skeleton rattle,' and we see all the moments of boredom and crisis, the lights and darks, all the joys and confusions of being young, of being alive."

— Ariel Gordon, author of *Stowaways,* winner of the 2015 Lansdowne Prize for Poetry

"Shirley Camia hangs her poems on the coat hooks of famous writers. The ones who respected children enough to show them the shortcut through the dark woods. Each poem, slight and vulnerable as a seven-year-old, examines the courage it takes to grow up. Illustrated by Cindy Mochizuki with evocative sketches, this book will haunt you with your own half-remembered past."

— Janet Trull, author of *Hot Town and Other Stories*

"This is a work to be read slowly. One must absorb the words, the visuals, the sensations and sentiments – ones that touch our most tender selves. The book uses poetry to link childhood readings and intimacies with tales that reveal truths in the most poignant way."

— Leanne Dunic, author of *To Love the Coming End*

Children Shouldn't Use Knives

and other tales

Children Shouldn't Use Knives

and other tales

Shirley Camia
with illustrations by Cindy Mochizuki

AT BAY press

WINNIPEG

Children Shouldn't Use Knives and Other Tales

Book design by Matthew Stevens.

Published by At Bay Press November 2017.

ISBN 978-1-988168-09-8

Library and Archives Canada cataloguing in publication is available upon request.

Typeset in Bookman Old Style and Bookman JF Pro.
Printed and bound in Canada.

This book is printed on acid free paper that is 100% recycled ancient-forest friendly (100% post-consumer recycled).

First Edition

atbaypress.com

10 9 8 7 6 5 4 3 2 1

for the authors on these pages

Contents

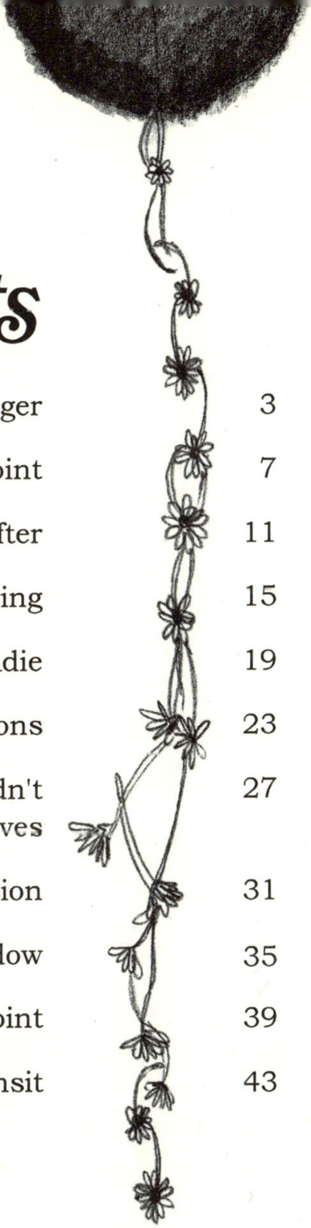

Children Shouldn't Use Knives

and other tales

I'm sorry to say so
but, sadly, it's true
that Bang-ups and Hang-ups
can happen to you.

- Dr. Seuss,
Oh, the Places You'll Go!

Stranger

a flock of trees
shadows the daylight

brings with it
shame
that cannot be fought

by a girl

when a stranger appears

There is a voice inside of you
That whispers all day long,
"I feel that this is right for me,
I know that *this* is wrong."

- Shel Silverstein,
Falling Up

Turning Point

what goes on inside a child's mind
in front of a strange man

who asks for her name
who calls her a bad girl
who tells her not to run
who asks what she can't mention
who drives off disgruntled
who undoes her trust

who says she is wrong

but

that voice

I know that's what people say—
you'll get over it. I'd say it, too.
But I know it's not true.

- Betty Smith,
A Tree Grows in Brooklyn

The Morning After

the dawn has a skeleton rattle

winter nags at her young bones
frozen from the blankets of sharp cold

carved blocks of hardened shadows

warmth haunts like a betrayal

She turned to the sunlight
And shook her yellow head,
And whispered to her neighbour:
"Winter is dead."

- A.A. Milne,
When We Were Very Young

In the Spring

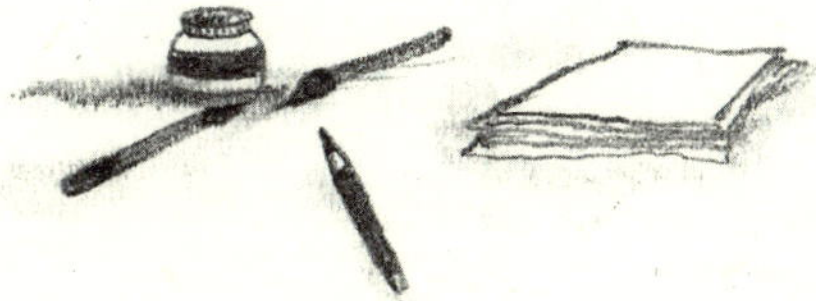

what defences
does a young
girl have

as anger
barrels down

the muzzle of a gun

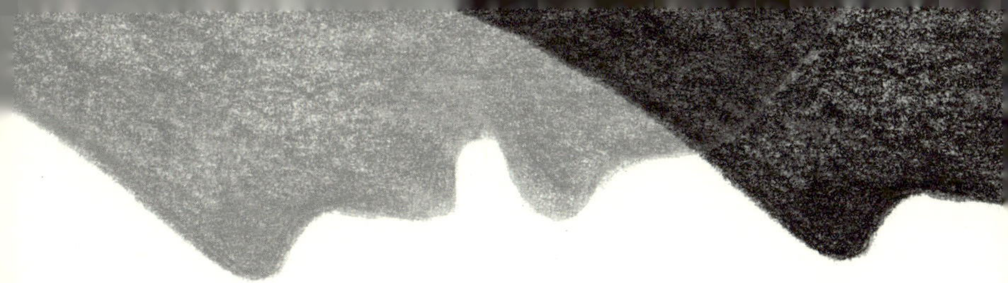

her tears form ponds

melting winter
down her dress

blood

"You have been my friend...
That in itself is a tremendous thing."

- E.B. White,
Charlotte's Web

19

Sadie

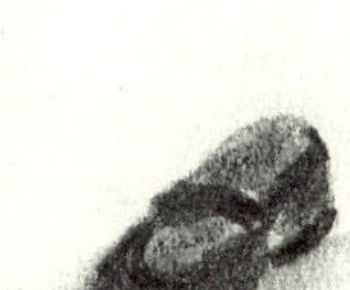

her blue dress flutters
like laundry
sideways and back
seduced by the charms of summer

a surrender
to the whims
of the wind

the air oozes salt and fresh lemons

in the worst drought in decades
the farmers say

the soil brittle
the grass yellow

specks of dust dance pirouettes

she struggles to finish her sundae
two scoops drowning in cherries
smeared and melting

drip
drip

down to her feet

sadie is the first to notice
her wet nose sniffing the
sweetness

she is 15

the years on her back
with the tumour

a weight
on her weakened legs

mother isn't ready

drip
drip

father starts the car

I don't understand it any more than
you do, but one thing I've learned is
that you don't have to understand
things for them to *be*.

- Madeleine L'Engle,
A Wrinkle in Time

Life Lessons

No, he's not here.
No, I haven't seen him.
No, I don't know where he is.

what she said
to the men
at the door

when she was eight

her uncle

down

the

stairs

Life is but a dream.

- Children's nursery rhyme,

"Row, Row, Row Your Boat"

Children Shouldn't Use Knives

under her father's snore
sesame street blares
then dies

the steady crescendos
of his afternoon nap

her blanket of boredom
thick

sleep distant

she sings herself into the kitchen
each note a tiptoe

row row row your boat

tickles of chilly air
breathing out the fridge door

gently down the stream

the flat steel
of the butter knife
the sweat
of the milk carton

merrily merrily

a slip

merrily merrily

darkness
pooling milk

life is but a dream...

And Max, the king of all wild things,
was lonely and wanted to be where
someone loved him best of all.

- Maurice Sendak,
Where the Wild Things Are

Exclusion

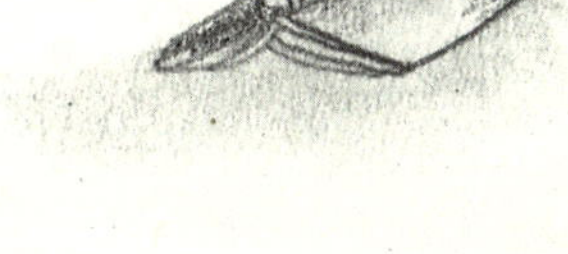

she can never hear the messages
untangled

behind cupped hands
to the ear

just a throb of tones
and giggles that

f l o a t

casually as smoke

her loneliness
filled

with the absence
of words
their song

and so much more

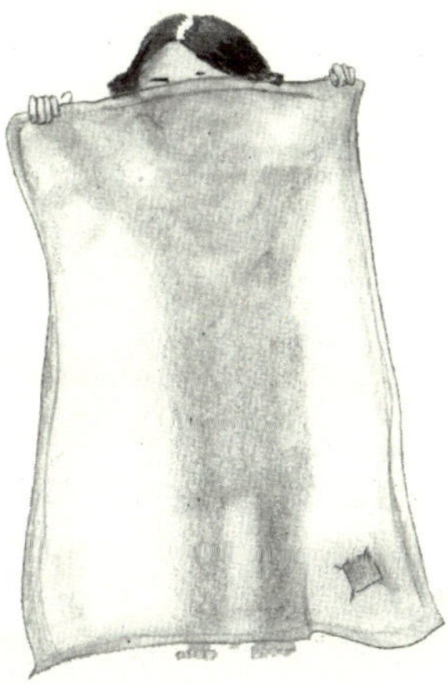

Are you there God?

- Judy Blume,

Are You There God? It's Me, Margaret

Through a Child's Window

stabs of sunlight
poke violently through

clouds

a parade of elephants
crossing an amber
traffic light
backwards

The books transported her into
new worlds and introduced her to
amazing people who lived exciting lives.
She went on olden-day sailing ships
with Joseph Conrad. She went to Africa
with Ernest Hemingway and to India
with Rudyard Kipling. She travelled all
over the world while sitting in her little
room...

- Roald Dahl,
Matilda

Past the Turning Point

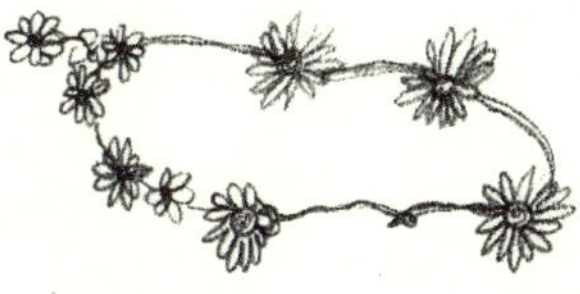

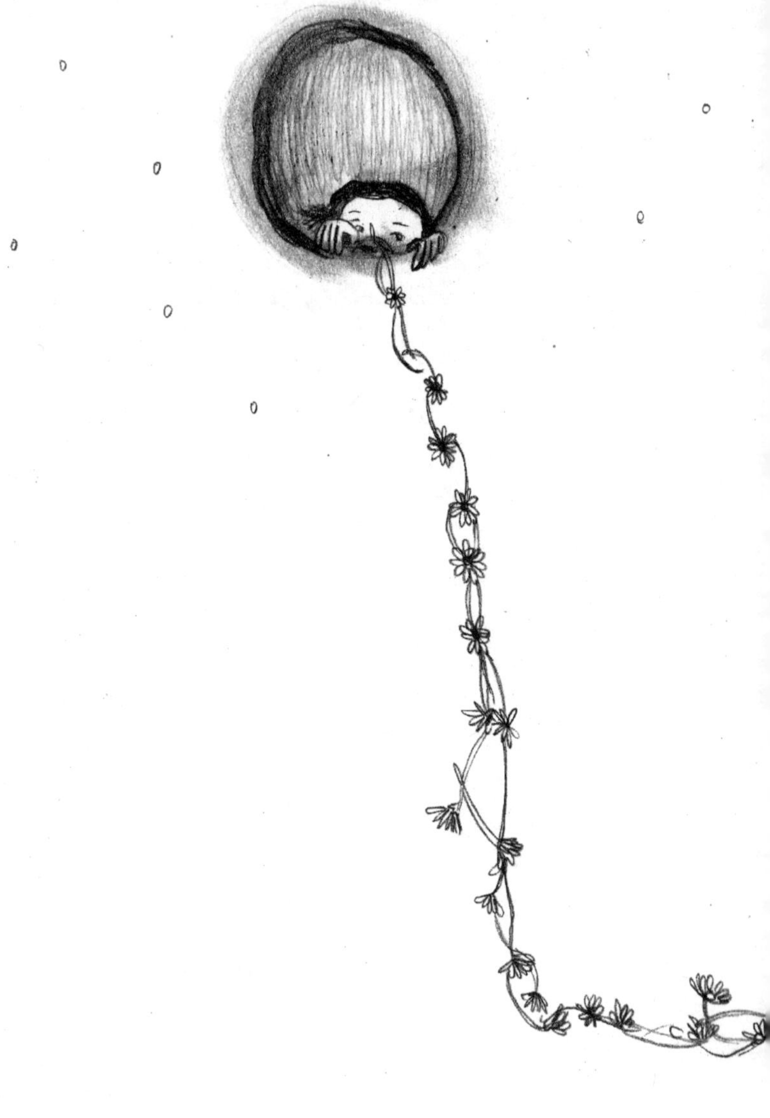

after the stranger
freedom comes in words

pages

the link
to the outside
world

denied to the child

for safety
for protection
for love

If you ever find yourself in
the wrong story, leave.

- Mo Willems,
Goldilocks and the Three Dinosaurs

In Transit

throw some dirt
on that place

a past beyond

and bury it

she won't be there long

her power
rising
with the edges of day

ablaze with the travelling dawn

ablaze

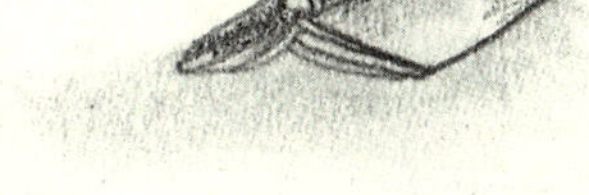

Acknowledgements

My deep gratitude to the people who brought this book to light:

Matt, Alana and the rest of the At Bay Press team for believing in this project and for seeing it through to the gorgeous hardcover that it is today.

Cindy Mochizuki for her strong yet delicate illustrations that made the poems in this book come to life.

Matt Stevens for his stellar graphic design work, for being open to suggestion and for connecting me with At Bay Press.

Robert Joseph for his critical eye.

Andy for his love and unwavering support.

Mom and Tatay for everything I have and I am.

And lastly, you, dear reader, for reading. Thank you.